Table of Contents

Chapter 3 – Picking the Project Team

- Getting the Right People
- Best Fit for the Role
- Best Fit for the Team
- Character
- Communicators
- Connectors
- Clarifying Roles
- Resource Planning
- Interviewing Considerations

Chapter 4 – Managing Diversity

- Organizational Culture
- Allocation of Financial Resources
- Favoritism
- Flexible Schedules
- Cultural Sensitivity
- Open Door Policy
- Problem Solving and Decision Making
- Stereotyping and Generalizing
- Training and Development
- Communication
- Accountability

Chapter 5 – Keeping the Team Inspired

- Goals
- Participation
- Positivity
- Be Part of the Team
- Milestones
- Allow Team to be in Control
- Recognition
- Remuneration
- Self-Development Opportunities
- Working Conditions

Chapter 6 – Positive Engagement Strategies

- Two-way Communication
- Active Listening
- Asking Questions
- Brain Storming
- Getting to Know Them

Conclusion

Introduction

I want to thank you and congratulate you for downloading the book, *"Project Management: The Beginner's Guide to Realizing Leadership Skills and Building Effective Teams"*.

This book contains proven steps and strategies on how to choose a great team for project work and how to walk your team through the stages of maturity until they become one effective machine made of different parts that work towards achieving the goals of the project.

In this eBook, we are going to look at not only how to build effective teams, but at how to bring out the best from everyone in that team. That sounds easy, but it can be a challenging job not withholding many rewards. As a leader, it will be your mandate to bring out the best in your team and to move them towards the success of the project.

We will also show you how to manage diversity. Your team will be made up of people from different generations; all of them have different ideas and beliefs. It is your duty to help them forge a way of working together so that they can bring the best in each other.

What are the stages that every team working together on a project must go through? There are many and we will discuss them in this eBook in detail.

Leaders are made. They are not born. They are made by everyday experiences. That is why everyday on the project must be a learning experience for you. As a leader, you can make or break the team. There is a thin line between success and failure.

This eBook has a wealth of ideas that can create and develop your leadership skills. However, it will not just happen. It will take hard work from you and consistent drive in the easy and tough times alike.

Bring out the best in your team and your project will come to fruition as intended upon inception. Work should be a pleasure, not a punishment. Do you have what it takes to venture this road of management?

Chapter 1

Do You Have the Key Competencies That a Manager Should Have?

You have been appointed the project manager. You are supposed to form a team and bring out the best in them. You do not know where to start; maybe you do not know how to spot the good qualities in people. Most importantly, you do not know what techniques to use to bring out the best in people.

It is hard selecting a great project team from many possible candidates, but it is not impossible. However, it will not just happen. You will have to do some footwork.

To be a good leader, firstly, you must know how to lead yourself. Secondly, you will be managing your project. Thirdly, you will be managing your team and fourthly, you will be managing the clients. That sounds like a big burden, but with a few smart project management techniques, you can have everything under control, neatly.

How?

Are you, as the manager, qualified to manage your team? Do you have the key competencies that are required to lead a project management team?

It takes a genius to recognize another genius. If you have the required qualities, you will also be able to recognize them easily when they are mirrored in another person. You can therefore see that becoming a good leader does not depend on the people that you are leading, but on you.

As a manager/leader, you must be able to determine the project goals first, so that you can sell them to the rest of the team easily. You will have to determine the appropriate parameters that you must set for yourself and the others in order to achieve the project objectives in time and within the budget.

Once you have set the parameters, you will then have to prioritize the project goals so that you can start on the most important ones first. You can apply the pyramid theory where the first priority is given to the most important aspect, following one another that way to the least important.

Finally, after prioritizing the goals, you will now have to coordinate the actual achievement of the goals to make sure that everything runs as planned.

The bottom line here is that unless you are a good leader to yourself, you cannot be a good leader for other people. That is why you need to explore yourself. Identify the relevant skills needed and nurturing them is a requirement to be a successful manager of people.

What are some of these skills? Here are a few questions that you should ask yourself:

1. Are you able to set high standards for yourself and to make sure that you meet them all the time? If not, then how can you be able to set targets for your team and follow up to make sure they meet them on time? You have to set standards for yourself before you can set them for other people.

2. How you communicate with your team is also very important. For example, do you dwell on

their weaknesses, or do you bring out the best in them?

From the book *Moving from Project Management to Project Leadership* by R. Camper Bull, he says that after the project is completed, you will not be remembered for what you did on your own, but for what you led your team to achieve. This also means that you should not hog all the glory once a job is done.

When you appreciate people for achieving goals, you build their strengths and confidence. When you criticize people for things that go wrong, you will be building their weaknesses.

Threaten, cajole, persuade, encourage, cheerlead and inspire – that is the work of a good leader, using every possible means to get a job done.

Communication is the baseline; it is the one most important quality that a team leader must possess. Without communication, many things can spiral out of control fast. Issues need to be resolved fast. Proper communication also ensures that there is no conflict of roles

3. Do you feel inspired? Do you understand the vision of the project? If you do not, how are you going to sell it to your team? If you know the vision of the project, you will then know the kind of talent it needs and thus, you will start on the right footing when you start recruiting talent for the project.

Scrutinize the project from all angles; see the end of the project from the beginning. Remember, your team will look up to you to give them inspiration and encouragement when challenges arise, and they will arise.

Do your research, your due diligence. Understand the project in detail. It starts with you. You are not a desk-general. You are a frontline general and you will lead your team from the front.

4. Do you command respect? Successfully managing people is an art form. People want to be directed without it being made too obvious that they are being ordered to do things. Thus, you should be convincing, friendly and at the same time, you should command respect. If something is not done right, do you hesitate to rectify this concern? If something is done to your expectations, do you give commendations?

Do people feel inspired by your presence? Do they look up to you to point the way, to lead them?

5. Can you keep in touch with people working on the project and give them appropriate feedback? This is very important. As a manager, you cannot afford not to communicate with the people working under you. Giving feedback will help correct mistakes and it will at the same time help the employees develop and utilize their full potential. You need to be a proactive communicator, address issues as soon as they arise so that they do not escalate or turn into habits.

6. Do you know how to manage a diverse team? Although we will handle this one later, the truth is that in today's workforce, there are diverse generations starting with the baby boomers, who are now exiting the workforce. There can be multiple different generations working on the same project. Some are in their 50s while some are in their early 20s. It can be a hard nut to crack bringing them together. All those diverse ideas when used well can make these employees very productive.

7. How can you polish your leadership skills? This is for you to find out. You see, leadership is not a one-off thing. Rather, it is an everyday lifestyle thing. Thus, we can say that once a leader, always a leader, and therefore you will need to keep on polishing your skills every day. Make every day a learning experience. That way, you will set the stage to be a leader who becomes better with time.

Take leadership resources, make use of them and take short leadership courses. The goal is to be a leader and a manager combined. Attend seminars, learn from the best leaders, see what they do, how they treat their employees and then adopt that.

8. How do you provide motivation and support? This is very important if you aim to bring out the best in the team working under you. As you start managing these people, you will learn that different people are motivated by different things. Some are motivated by praise, others are motivated by cash bonuses, others

by public recognition and yet others by promotions.

Find out what motivates every person in your team, and then follow it up with the relevant rewards.

Know the people who work under you on a personal level. That way, you can be able to identify and tackle morale problems as soon as you realize that something is amiss. Know your team!

Conclusion

These are just a few of attributes that you need to have as a leader. There are many more, but among them all, the most important ones are these. There is nothing like an accomplished leader. Leadership is a learning experience, something that you grow every day.

Chapter 2

The Project Planning Stage - Laying the Foundation

Project work can be hefty, unless you start everything on a good foundation. That is why at this stage, even before you can go selecting the team to work with, you and other leaders can lay the foundation of the project. However, there is also merit in having your team selected first so that everybody can start the project on the same note.

In this stage where you lay the foundation for the project, there are many concepts involved. However, here, we have categorized them into three to make things easier for you. By recognizing these different concepts, a manager can begin to conceptualize in their mind how the project will move forward.

In the earliest stages of the project foundation, experts recommend that you form a team for the job. This is the forming stage. You will be forming a team, selecting the people that you would like to work with on that project.

Here are the three stages of laying the foundation:

   a) Forming

   b) Storming

   c) Norming

And then there are the final two stages for the completion of the project:

   d) Performing

   e) adjourning

The Forming Stage

The team that you select can make or break the project. It is the single most important determining factor when it comes to project success. Therefore, you need to choose your team carefully. Learning how to identify and select talent is something anybody can learn.

Here are a few things to know and do:

1. The team that you choose will be made up of people who will go through a few stages of getting to know each other, getting used to each other's different style of working, adapting to each other until eventually, they will form a formidable team, a well synchronized team working towards achieving the same goal.

2. Your duty as the manager is to understand what you need to do so that you can make your team one effective machine. This is very important if you are looking for the best outcomes.

3. Remember, at the forming stage the team is timid, since they are not used to each other and they are still learning how to handle one another.

4. At this stage, the team does not know what is expected of them. They do not understand their roles exactly and therefore you have to be patient. It is your duty to make sure that everyone understands perfectly what is expected of them. This is also the time to encourage questions so that you can ensure

that every person knows what is expected of them.

5. Even though you have a time limit in mind, remember that this period can spread out a bit and therefore you should be patient with the team. Let them learn how to work with each other. However, be sure to iron out any differences that may arise between these people. Usually, when you have explained the goal of the project effectively, there should be few problems since everyone will know that the part they will play in the project will be important in the achievement of the final goal.

6. If you are going to form small teams within the bigger team, this is the stage where you do it. At this stage, the team members are going to express their wishes, their desires and most importantly, what they bring to the table. Based on their skills and experiences, you can know whom to pair with whom to form great teams.

As they introduce themselves, they will also form alliances immediately, you know, that first time feeling when people they can work together. Mostly, these early alliances will last until the project is over.

But first, they have to survive the storming stage

The Storming Stage

This is where most teams do break apart, but don't worry. With careful planning and deliberation, that is not going to happen to your team. This is also the stage where the team gets to push the boundaries and see what can happen and who will emerge on top.

Just as the name suggests, at this stage, all the members of the team will be trying to bring out their best, and since everyone will be trying to outdo everyone else, there are bound to be 'storms.'

These people are still not used to one another and therefore there will be conflicts. However, at this stage, you need to quell such chaos swiftly by making sure that all arising issues are solved amicably. Give them your guidance and tell them you expect them to work together. The most important thing here is not to like each other, but to learn to work even with people that they do not like for the common good of the project.

Here is what you can do as the team leader to assist your team to get through this stage:

1. Create some time everyday where the team members can vent and bring out all issues that arose during the day.

2. Address the issues that they bring up one by one. Nothing, no matter how mundane it seems should be left pending. This ensures that by the following day, everyone is on the same page.

3. The main thing that you have to do at this stage is to encourage teamwork. If you do not teach them how to solve issues and determine solutions as a team, you will lose them forever. Do not let that happen. Be smart. You should not take chances.

4. Whenever you are holding a discussion as a team, be a smart moderator and do not allow any one person to dominate the discussion with opinions, ideas and so on. Give everyone, even the timid ones a fair chance to be heard. You will be surprised that sometimes, the people who talk the least are the best.

5. Know when to close the stage. As soon as you realize that the team has started working together, compliment them and let them know that you are soon moving over to the next stage.

Be careful here; do not limit time too much. Give them time to learn to work as a team. Many project leaders have moved their teams from this stage too soon, only for them to realize later in the project that the people they are leading are still in the storming stage. Do not allow that to happen. Be a good judge. If they are not ready, tell them so and insist that you need more effort from them.

Many teams work through the entire project while still in this stage. They never outgrow it and therefore they proceed through the other stages in chaos and this hampers the progress of the project a great deal.

It is better to root out people whom you find to be emotional and immature at this stage, rather than proceed with them and regret it later. No chances should be taken at this stage. From here, you should only proceed with people who are ready to form a solid team.

The norming stage

Congratulations! If you have gotten your team this far, then you deserve much more than just a pat on the back.

By virtue of having made it beyond the storming stage, well, the storm is now over. Now is your time to shine – your team is now working like a well-oiled machine and you can reap the rewards of your previous efforts.

Many teams do not make it past the storming stage, but yours has. Now, things will be clearer, the work will progress faster, and the team, while they are not exactly buddies, has learnt to work together. The morale and motivation are high and this can be used to leverage further successes and to build momentum. There is no superiority or inferiority complexes at play, well, I lied, there are, but they are nothing that you cannot handle.

This is the stage where the stormy seas start calming and by this stage, the team is united. It is a team; the members can accommodate opinions different from their own. The battles for supremacy are over; team leaders have been chosen and everyone is ready to follow the regulations.

When you get to the storming stage, the team is very mature by now and they start appreciating the values that their diversity adds to the project. Respect is given both ways, from the leaders to the team and vice versa.

The team agrees on the rules of working together, rules that will not be violated and which everyone is comfortable with. They agree even on the methods of solving conflicts as well as the ways in which they will manage their differences.

As the team leader, you will now have more free time on your hands for other things, because at this point, you will find that the team does not really need you to solve their disputes or to supervise them. This team is mature.

Stick around though, pop in from to time and see to it that everything is moving along nicely. You see, many times, there will be differences and at times, the diversity could be a problem. All negative energy must be let out. Just be there to get these people in line if they deviate.

The most important thing right now is to ensure that the entire team has the goals of the project in focus. For that, you are no longer just a leader. You are now a coach. You are pointing out the direction for the team and you are leading from the front. By the time you are done with this stage, these people can head their own project teams, well, almost.

The performing stage

The hurdles have long been overcome. If you have come this far, no doubt the project is running along nicely. You are happy, the clients are happy, your seniors are happy and the team is happy.

The performing stage is where the team performs as a single organism, yet with so many different aspects that are nevertheless headed towards achieving the same goals for the project. No supervision is needed here, everyone is sure of what they are supposed to do every day.

Because many project management teams do not make it to this stage, well, you can be sure that getting to the performing stage is quite something. The team solves conflicts easily, without any issues, and most importantly, they are working as a team.

Now, what you need to do as the manager is to make sure that the team does not revert to any of the earlier stages. That would be easy, in case there arises issues that they overestimate. However, as long as they are solving issues without affecting the progress of the project, well, the danger of reverting to the latter stages is minimal.

Know the things that could force the team to revert to an older stage and then know how to manage such. For example, at this stage, if one member quits the team, well, that could affect the team greatly, as would the coming in of a new member.

The adjourning stage

This is the summit. The team is almost done and some members have already left or are preparing to leave to go back to their old jobs. The project is by now completed, and the outcome of the project as been determined. This can take months or years depending upon the mandate and nature of the project.

Make sure that you prepare for a proper exit by arranging a party where you can recognize the team members individually for everything that they have done.

Appraise the entire project:

- Was it a success?
- What lessons have you all learned in the project?
- If the project failed, what made it fail?

It is goodbye time. The most likely thing is that everyone who made it to this stage will want to keep in touch with the other team members, as they will most likely want to work on more projects in future.

Arrange for a proper dignified exit, with time for everyone to wish each other well in their future endeavors.

Chapter 3

Picking Your Project Team - Getting the Right People

First, congratulations for having been appointed the project manager. After a moment of celebration, you now need to get to work and the first thing you are supposed to do is get the right people to form your project team.

In fact, your success or failure relies entirely on the project team that you are going to pick. This therefore means that there is only one option for you – to pick the most qualified and motivated people.

This crucial step might feel overwhelming and you may not know where to start. Just like hiring, picking the right people for your project team is actually an art and a science. It is not going to be an easy task, but it is not impossible. But how do you go about it?

Because you need the right people on your team, you should ask yourself who the right people are and what characteristics the best project teams should possess.

Generally, the right people are the ones who:

- Genuinely want to be on the project
- Have the necessary skills to properly undertake and complete the project
- Have adequate time available to focus on the job at hand

If you consider the above characteristics, you will be picking people based on passion, ability and capacity to best compliment the project's success. In this way, you will have chosen the best team for your project.

When you already know the skills needed to complete the project, you should also consider some intangibles that will influence the way your project team is going to function. If you know these aspects and put them into consideration while you are picking your project team, you will be able to have everything under control.

What are these aspects? Well, here are the five key ones that you must take into account:

Best fit for the role

When you are filling the role's requirements, you should consider the knowledge, ability and skill of the candidate. Of course, you do not want to hire a physicist who doesn't have any bookkeeping skills to do an account's job.

This is where the issue of experience fits and as a project manager, you should ask and give yourself an appropriate answer to this question: Should I pick an enthusiastic but less experienced candidate, or do I pick a jaded veteran who clearly possesses the skills?

Best fit for your team

As a leader, your task is to identify people who are committed to your project and compatible with other team members. Keep away from picking the "yes-men and –women" but instead, look for those people who can voice a completely different perspective from you or from other team members.

Sometimes, all that the team needs is a fresh point of view. Again, the right people for any project are results-oriented who come in to make a difference.

Character

When getting people for your project team take into account a candidate's character and make sure the team is full of positive personalities. Taking on a project is not the easiest of tasks and the situation can get worse when you are working with people who have negative personalities.

Look for people with integrity who will take responsibility for their tasks and actions. These are the greatest assets to your team. Go for candidates who are coachable/teachable and who possess a mentoring attitude to encourage teamwork. As a project team leader, you need an environment where every member becomes a mentor and a mentee.

Communicators

As expected, your team will have issues along the way. So, when you're picking your team, you should look for people who will not clam up defensively. Instead, look for people who will talk about issues that will be affecting the smooth running of the project.

Nothing is healthier than good communication because it helps you face and fix problems prior to them becoming out of control. Again, good communication helps a great deal when it comes to uniting a team. In that way, the team will work positively toward a common goal, which leads to success.

Connectors

As much as you are supposed to be positive, you should be realistic as well. Like any other successful project manager, you should expect your project to hit a rough spot, or a few of them along the way. This is where you need team members with good internal influence especially if you are working for a large organization.

If you recruit connectors in your team, they will know where to find internal resources and how to get things done even when the project is facing challenges.

After you have identified the right candidates, the next step is to interview them.

You should keep the following in mind:

Be clear about roles

As a project manager, you should create roles as early as when you are interviewing a candidate. Unclear or overlapping roles often create conflict later, which can actually affect your project negatively. Discuss and agree about responsibilities, tasks and goals before you hire a candidate.

Create a resource plan

Make use of tools such as online project management software to identify the skills you need for the project and how many hours should be involved.

Prepare clear hypothetical questions

You actually want to learn how your prospective team members think. Therefore, prepare hypothetical questions that you are going to ask them. Ask them the questions that present hypothetical situations that are likely to come up in your project. Present them with different types of questions and scenarios that represent different roles.

Lastly, resist the temptation to hire clones of yourself but instead, look for team members with different skills and personalities. Remember that the whole process is all about finding the right person for your team. Bringing together complementary skills and personalities will attribute to the team's potential and the overall success of the project.

Chapter 4

Managing Diversity and Differences Among People of the Same Team

The workplace is a diverse community of workers, just as all the other institutions or communities are, including the home. People from different backgrounds come together for a specific reason of achieving the goals of the organization they work for.

These differences include culture, age, race, gender, and even physical ability. Inability to manage diversity can have disastrous results. These include low employee morale, high staff turnover, and absenteeism, which lead to low productivity.

Consequently, understanding these people and leading them requires the use of strategies that promote respect amongst them. It is also important to avoid discrimination of any person. Managers who succeed in getting the best out of diverse teams develop a competitive edge, thus become leaders in their respective industries.

Given that most businesses rely on a diverse team for survival, the following actions can help to steer your team on the path to accomplishing your set goals.

A few ways for managing diversity

Organizational culture – Project teams with diverse skills, opinions, races, genders and even beliefs should emphasize diversity as an overriding cultural value. This means that the culture of the organization values and respects employees irrespective of their background.

The culture should also focus on the high standards of every employee. Both men and women ought to be treated equally, and their performances measured equally.

Everybody should always be treated the same way and given access to the same resources. This builds a sense of equality, thus promoting harmony within the diverse team.

Allocation of financial resources – Diversity management comes with a number of costs. These costs include training expenses for both managers and the people reporting to them.

Avoid favoritism – It is not advisable to treat some members of your team better than others. You should try to understand each member, but not give undue attention to particular members of the team. This applies even when you are brainstorming on the round table. Give everyone a fair chance to speak.

Flexible schedules – People from diverse backgrounds have diverse needs. These include different prayer times, days of worship, or even dress code. It is good to allow people some freedom in relation to their unique wants.

Pregnant mothers also ought to be allowed to work on a flexible schedule, thus help them meet their unique needs. Using such strategies improves productivity in your team as you make the team motivated to do their best.

Be culturally sensitive – teams consist of different people from different cultural backgrounds. Understanding the culture of your team members enables you to handle them properly, and reduce unnecessary conflicts. It is wise to value individual differences, and appreciate that people have different beliefs.

Maintain an open door policy – This makes it easy for your team to get to you, and discuss issues that could be bothering them. Such discussions make it easy to solve problems that could affect employee morale. It also gives way to constructive conflict as problems can be discussed and be solved for the benefit of the organization.

Inclusive problem solving and decision-making – participation of the entire team allows you to capitalize on the strengths of the different employees, which makes them feel valued. More to that, the employees gain a sense of belonging, thus being committed to the organization.

Avoid stereotyping and generalizing – We are all brought up differently, and we have been socialized differently. We hold different biases towards varying groups of people. However, if you are to manage a diverse team, you need to get rid of your biases and prejudices against others. This requires you to dismiss myths related to diverse persons when leading a diverse team.

Training and development – Good leaders take time to educate themselves about the diverse culture of different employees. Training also exposes leaders to the different beliefs and myths of their diverse team, which promotes their ability to handle different employees.

Moreover, diversity management is all about your team. Making them aware of the impact of diversity can make it easy for you to manage diversity. Training them about diversity helps them to understand and appreciate the benefits of working together.

It promotes an environment of mutual trust, empowerment, and teamwork, which encourages your team to be a community.

Communication – Communication is the backbone of any successful team. Managers ought to communicate effectively with their employees. As a team leader, listen carefully to your employees. Encourage questions when they do not understand. This minimizes conflicts in their team.

Use of satisfaction surveys can also help managers to get sensitive information. All employees can, for instance, be asked to fill in surveys that focus on diversity issues. Results from the surveys can then be used to implement an effective diversity policy.

Informal channels also help in getting vital information that can be used to manage a diverse team. Websites or chat rooms, for example, give employees a platform where they can share their ambitions, as well as grievances.

Such communication improves socialization among your team members, thus fostering the spirit of togetherness. It also makes it easy to solve problems and introduce changes that can improve diversity.

Accountability – This involves being at the forefront of promoting diversity. A leader needs to show that they value diversity by giving attention to the diverse opinions of his team. They should also promote non-discriminatory acts and always ensure equality among all employees.

Managers can also promote diversity by recruiting leaders who represent diverse teams in the top positions. Such leaders depict an all-inclusive organization, thus promoting the success of a diverse team.

Chapter 5

10 Tips to Inspire your Project Team

Keeping your project team inspired plays a significant role in the success of your project. Inspired employees have greater capacity to yield the expected results, unlike demoralized employees.

Motivated employees are not only accountable, but also bearers of your projects' vision. Therefore, inspiring your team is a responsibility that when done properly ensures that your team exceeds the expected results. You can accomplish team inspiration by using several options as this eBook outlines.

How to inspire your team

1. Have clear goals

When working with a project team it is important for you to set clear goals. Clear goals motivate your team, making them work well on the project. This results from the fact that clear goals give a sense of direction. The goals allow your team to know what should be done next. They know what they should expect at every stage of the project. The team also knows the expected results, which ensures that they work towards achieving the set goals.

2. Treasure the participation of the whole team

It feels good when people listen to you or even implement your suggestions. Therefore, allowing your team to participate in the decision making process of your project can inspire them.

It gives them a sense of belonging, which motivates them to work on the project as if it was their personal responsibility. Therefore, always listen to your team and implement their suggestions whenever possible.

3. Maximize positivity

Handle every challenge with a positive attitude. Your team will follow your lead if you seek to find possibilities where the impossibilities tend to dominate. By encouraging your team to keep on trying, despite the challenges that may make them despair. Therefore, if you want to inspire your team, eliminate the negative thinking that says things are going wrong.

You refrain from looking down on every failure of your team members. These are merely learning opportunities. You can choose to accept when your employees fail, and work with them on correcting their mistakes or you can disempower them through micromanagement. Act correctly as a true leader and empower your team through these opportunities.

4. Be part of the team

Work on any area of the project that you are capable of handling. This shows your team that you are also committed to the success of the project. They get inspired when they see you working towards the success of the project, thus encouraging them to work with you towards achievement of the project goals.

5. Discuss milestones of the project regularly

It is wise to have frequent meetings with your team where you discuss the progress of the project. This can be weekly or fortnight meetings, depending on the nature of the project. During such meetings, clearly indicate the development of the project.

Discuss whether the project is on track and give guidance on the consecutive steps that are still ahead. On the other hand, do not hold meetings that do not add value to your project. Only hold meetings that discuss important issues, as opposed to meetings that waste your project time. Never hold a meeting just to hold a meeting – and remember, could what you're meeting about be better communicated by email?

6. Allow your team to be in control

Make your team feel in charge of the work that you have given them. They should know that you are not there to issue them orders. Instead, they should feel responsible for the tasks they do and the outcome of the project.

They ought to know that they own the project and their actions dictate the success of the project. This means you should avoid micromanaging your team members. Do not exert too much control over them. Instead, allow them to develop their own ways of achieving their clear-cut duties.

7. Recognize individual efforts

When you recognize and reward individual effort, people get more motivated unlike when you recognize team effort. Acknowledging individuals makes them more enthusiastic, and they work tirelessly to accomplish project goals.

Motivated individuals give you a motivated team, which emphasizes the need for inspiring employees individually. Build on individual strengths, and help weak individuals to perfect their skills.

8. Remunerate your team properly

Paying your team well inspires them to work on the project. Always ensure that you pay them what they are worth. This helps to avoid staff departure, which can affect your project adversely.

It is good to pay your team the equivalent of what your industry offers to similar employees. This way, your team remains competitive, and does not waste project time searching for alternative jobs.

9. Value self-development

Employees do not only want to work for you for a pay at the end of the month. Most employees appreciate an opportunity to grow their skills. They would be more motivated if you gave them a chance to learn a new skill, thus advance their career profile. You should also remember that promoting their skills not only promotes their knowledge. It also increases their ability to give your project the best.

10. Good working conditions

We all deserve to work in comfortable and pleasant places. Provide your project team with a good office. The office should, for example, have enough space for your team to avoid congestion. The office furniture should be of good quality.

For project work, get the right tech tools like project management software, good computers and so on. Good equipment motivates the team to work to peak productivity all the time.

Chapter 6

Making People Feel Encouraged, Wanted and Appreciated

As a project manager, you play a vital leadership role in ensuring that your team works to achieve the success of the project. After investing time, effort and monetary resources to pick the best people for your team, it is everyone's guess that the last thing you want is to lose anyone of them.

Without motivation, skills are nothing

Chances are that the people you picked know exactly what they are supposed to do to complete the project successfully. Your teammates are highly competent and efficient at what they do. However, you should understand that without motivation, they are not going to deliver as they should even with their excellent skills.

Motivation causes people to behave right and achieve more

When you have motivated people around you, your team will achieve more. Apart from their direct contribution, encouraged people will set the standard in attitude, behavior as well as results for everybody else. Simply put, motivated people are the most valuable assets for your project.

As a project manager, you have a responsibility to make these people feel encouraged, wanted and appreciated. This makes them very happy and motivated. In the same way, your team and the project at large will benefit from the exceptional performance of each person.

If you notice signs that some people or the entire team feel that they are not wanted, appreciated or encouraged, you should take it very seriously and address the issue as soon as possible because if you don't, chances are that your project is not going to be successful.

It takes a leader to understand that it is critical to keep valued team members motivated, effective and engaged. So, where do you start? How can you make them feel encouraged, wanted and appreciated?

Well, here is what you should do:

1. Encourage two-way communication

Traditional, information used to flow from top to bottom, you know, orders being issued from the top dog. That has changed today. As a leader, communication is at the core of your project success. First, you need to spend your time communicating with the various project constituents and then encourage the communication among team members.

Communication represents that link, which binds together all the pieces of the project. And together, all team members involved with the project will enjoy its success.

By achieving small goals of the project along the way when there is effective communication, every team member feels like he/she has made meaningful contribution. This makes them feel encouraged wanted and appreciated.

To encourage two-way communication, you can do the following:

2. Active listening

If you want to motivate people, you must encourage active listening because effective communication is supposed to be a two-way street. On your side, you must ensure that you listen carefully to your team members when they speak.

Always make sure you are not getting ready to reply but instead, listen to understand them. Otherwise, you might miss an important detail. In this way, your teammates will feel motivated in a very big way. In the same way, you should encourage active listening among your teammates.

3. Ask questions

When you are discussing something with people, ask them questions when you hear anything that confuses you. Again, you might miss something during the conversation and to avoid misunderstanding, ask questions for clarification.

Because effective communication must be a two-way affair, encourage others to ask you questions and give them humble time to understand everything that they want to know concerning the project. This way, people will feel happy and motivated more than you can imagine.

4. Hold regular brainstorming sessions

Your project will have issues along the way. You did not for one moment think that it would be smooth sailing all the way, did you?

Whenever your project has any thorny issues, the best thing to do is to turn to brainstorming. Without wasting time, you should get together with your team and frame the problem before determining a solution together.

Call out for different ideas from your teammates and then build on each other's ideas. Brainstorming does not only solve problems that the project is facing, but it also makes people feel motivated in a great way.

Brainstorming with a group of team members is a powerful technique. Apart from creating new ideas, it solves problems and develops teams. Above all, it motivates because it involves all the members of your project team. By working together as a team, people feel encouraged, wanted and appreciated in a big way, which makes them complete the project successfully.

Keep away from conducting brainstorming as a simple random activity. If you do that, you might solve your project problem but some of your team members might feel unappreciated or unworthy.

Structure your brainstorming and follow its rule. Otherwise, you will not achieve its goals. Because brainstorming needs to involve the entire team, every person is supposed to see what is happening.

5. Know them at some personal level

Nothing motivates people more than knowing that others, especially their seniors, know about them. Of course, you want to show your team members that you care, and you value them.

When you are addressing the team, make sure you address them directly by calling their real names. Even when you meet in a corridor, call a person with his or her name and in that way, they will know that you know, care about and remember them.

Keep reminders of their birthdays so that you surprise them with a gift or a team party. People will take it very passionately when you can remember their birthdays. Seek for more information about their lives and know important things like their anniversaries so that you can recognize their most important days in life.

Conclusion

Thank you again for downloading this eBook!

I hope this was able to help you to bring out the very best in your project team. I also hope that it has helped you become a better leader.

The next step now is to put into practice everything that you have learned from this eBook. Also, make it a point to carry out more research to see how you can bring out the best from your team.

Whether the project is a success or a failure, if you kept the team together beyond the storming stage (remember chapter 2?) well, you have done well, and in some way, the team was a great success.

Again, thank you for your time – it is truly a limited resource. I would be very appreciative if you could drop by Amazon and leave a kindle review to help other people find this resource. If you have any suggestions for further books please do suggest them!

Before you go...

If you enjoyed this read and feel that others could benefit from it please feel free to leave a review. They help me reach a wider audience! Thank you and good luck in your journey!

www.ingramcontent.com/pod-product-compliance
Lightning Source LLC
Chambersburg PA
CBHW070420190526
45169CB00003B/1348